ROBERT SCHUMANN

OVERTURE
SHAKESPEARE'S
JULIUS CAESAR
OUVERTURE ZU
SHAKESPEARES
JULIUS CÄSAR

Op. 128

Edited by/Herausgegeben von
Armin Koch

Ernst Eulenburg Ltd

London · Mainz · Madrid · New York · Paris · Prague · Tokyo · Toronto · Zürich

CONTENTS

Critical edition based on
Robert Schumann. New Edition of the Complete Works
Volume I/3
© 2013 Schott Music, Mainz
RSA 1010, ISMN 979-0-001-15592-2
Reprinted by permission

© 2014 Ernst Eulenburg & Co GmbH, Mainz
for Europe excluding the British Isles
Ernst Eulenburg Ltd, London
for all other countries

Ernst Eulenburg Ltd
48 Great Marlborough Street
London W1F 7BB

PREFACE

Robert Schumann composed altogether nine complete works for orchestra with the title 'overture'. On his own initiative most of these were also performed and published independently or were at least destined for performance and publication. The majority specifically feature in the title an extra-musical subject or a musical reference. Special cases constitute the early attempt *Ouverture et Chor* of 1822/23 (*RSW* Appendix I9, not published by Schumann) and the *Ouverture, Scherzo und Finale* Op.52. The latter is the only overture without specific external reference.

Three of the overtures are connected with larger works: the opera *Genoveva* Op.81, *Manfred* Op.115, referred to by Schumann as a 'Dramatic Poem', together with the *Scenen aus Goethes Faust* ['Scenes from Goethe's Faust'] (WoO 3, posthumously published). The composer himself had also had the overtures for *Genoveva* (originated in 1847, published in 1850) and *Manfred* (originated in 1848, published in 1852) published and performed as autonomous works, both of which he had composed in advance of the rest of each respective work. In this regard there are no specific references for the *Faust-Scenen* overture, the last section of that work to be composed. Three further overtures composed within merely a year are handed down without reference to a larger work – as is also the *Fest-Ouverture mit Gesang über das Rheinweinlied* ['Festival Overture with Song on the Rhine Wine Lied'] Op.123 – and are thus to be viewed purely as concert overtures. Two of them preceded, in fact, deliberations for composing an opera or *Liederspiel* (*Ouverture zur Braut von Messina von Fr. v. Schiller* ['Overture to the Bride of Messina by Fr. v. Schiller'] Op.100, composed at the end of 1850/start of 1851, published in 1851, and *Ouverture zu Goethes Hermann und Dorothea* ['Overture to Goethe's Hermann and Dorothea'], composed at the end of 1851, published posthumously as

Op.136). No other kinds of musical sources are known, however, to supplement the overtures. For the *Ouverture zu Shakespeares Julius Cäsar* ['Overture to Shakespeare's Julius Caesar'] Op.128 (composed in spring 1851, published in 1854/55) no such deliberations are documented. The *Rheinweinlied* overture differs categorically from the other overtures since it – composed as a Festival Overture for the Lower Rhenish Musical Festival in 1853 – belongs to another genre.

A diary entry of Clara Schumann's about her husband stems from the period when the overture to the *Braut von Messina* was composed:[1] 'The idea to write overtures to several of the most beautiful tragedies had so excited him that his genius again overflowed with music.' In the so-called *Düsseldorfer Merkbuch*, Schumann recorded besides a longer series of tragedies, also – as he wrote in a letter[2] – a list for a 'cycle of overtures':[3] as numbers 1–4 are those to *Genoveva, Braut von Messina, Julius Cäsar* and *Manfred*. Limiting the subject of the 'cycle' to tragedies was never explicitly suggested, and hence Schumann could later add as number 5 the overture to *Hermann und Dorothea*. The plan though was not realised.

On the Present Work

Robert Schumann composed the *Ouverture zu Shakespeare's Julius Cäsar* ['Overture to Shakespeare's Julius Caesar'] Op.128 within a few

---

[1] Berthold Litzmann, *Clara Schumann. Ein Künstlerleben. Nach Tagebüchern und Briefen*, Vol.II: *Ehejahre 1840–1856* (Leipzig ,⁶1920), 259
[2] Schumann's letter to C.F.Peters, 24 March 1851, Heinrich-Heine-Institut, Düsseldorf; Accessions-No.: *91.5045/1*. Schumann's correspondence with Peters is published in: *Briefwechsel Robert und Clara Schumanns mit Leipziger Verlegern III*, eds. Petra Dießner, Irmgard Knechtges-Obrecht and Thomas Synofzik (Cologne, 2008: *Schumann Briefedition*, III/3).
[3] *Robert Schumann. Düsseldorfer Merkbuch*, Robert-Schumann-Haus, Zwickau; Archives-No.: *4871,VII,C,7–A3,* 7

days.[4] He began the draft on 23 January 1851 and finished the score on 2 February,[5] less than three weeks after he had completed his overture to Friedrich Schiller's *Braut von Messina* ['The Bride of Messina'] Op. 100. Whereas the latter was demonstrably prompted by thoughts of a possible opera subject, no such motivation is known for the overture to Shakespeare's *Julius Caesar.*

Schumann had first planned the overture for the 1851/52 winter concert season,[6] but then did not perform it. Instead, the work was played in the 'Large Vocal and Instrumental Concert' on the third day of the Düsseldorf 'Great Song Festival' (1–4 August 1852).[7] Schumann's health was very poor at this time. His brother-in-law Woldemar Bargiel, whom Schumann had commissioned to prepare the piano arrangement for four hands, used the rehearsals as well as the performance to become better acquainted with the work. In his diary of the summer 1852 Bargiel recorded for the first day of rehearsal, 30 July:[8]

Finally, the musicians were assembled for the rehearsal; the orchestra was still very poorly staffed and many instruments were entirely missing, meantime, however, it went better than I had imagined; after the third time the Beethoven overture Op. 124 sounded really presentable, the Sch[umann] though a bit muddled, and only in the end as Sch.[umann] himself conducted did it become reasonably coherent. Tausch had conducted at first and I must confess that he did [not?] seem to have entirely grown into the job. The *Cäsar* overture had made a powerful impression on me and I dare not criticize anything in it, for the striking places are just those met with in the invention, and a superficial opinion about it deserves to be disputed at once; it will certainly produce the most magnificent effect. Sch[umann], who first listened to his overture along with us, could at last not keep himself from taking baton in hand, and I was pleased with what circumspection and energy he conducted, but still more that meantime it seemed to have made him completely well, because I met him in the best mood at the evening meal, so I would like the festival days to pass under his direction.

The review in the *Berliner Musik-Zeitung Echo* of 15 August 1852 supposed generally an inadequate preparation of the orchestra as well as an inequality of winds and strings and especially criticised the orchestra.[9] Completely different was the extensive review of the song festival in the music journal *Signale für die musikalische Welt* a few days later, on 19 August. The emphasis on the precise execution and the mention of the problematical acoustics of the provisionally built *Tonhalle* indicate not least that the report was reacting to the criticism of the *Berliner Musik-Zeitung Echo*.[10]

Editorial Notes[11]

Except for a draft in short-score form as well as a crossed-out inscription of the flute part comprising only a few bars, no manuscript sources are extant. The engraver's models sent to Henry Litolff, owner of the G.M.Meyer publishing house in Braunschweig, on 14 September 1853[12] evidently remained in the publishing house and are lost. Relevant for the present edition are the extant sources:

[4] There is a detailed presentation of the 'History of the Work' in the volume of the Complete Edition *Robert Schumann. Neue Ausgabe sämtlicher Werke*, Series I, Work Group 3 (RSA I/3) with the orchestral versions of the overtures, 339–362

[5] See *Robert Schumann. Projectenbuch*, Robert-Schumann-Haus, Zwickau; Archives-No.: *4871,VII,C,8–A3*, 59

[6] See *Düsseldorfer Merkbuch*, 21

[7] See *Städtischer Männergesangverein zu Düsseldorf. GROSSES GESANGFEST. GESANGWETTSTREIT, COMPOSITIONSKAMPF, Concert und Grosses Künstlerfest der Gesellschaft Malkasten am 1., 2., 3. und 4. August 1852. Programm und Fest-Ordnung. Ehrenpreise, Texte der Gesänge, Namens-Verzeichniss sämmtlicher Mitwirkenden* (Düsseldorf, [1852]).

[8] Robert-Schumann-Haus, Zwickau; Archives-No.: *2008.037– A3*, entry for 30 July 1852, [31–34]

[9] See '– W. –', 'Das Sänger- und Musikfest in Düsseldorf am 1–3. August d. J.', in: *Berliner Musik-Zeitung Echo*, Vol.2, No.33, 15 August 1852, 259–261, especially 259f.

[10] Anon. [= Wilhelm Joseph von Wasielewski], 'Das Düsseldorfer Gesangfest', in: *Signale*, Vol.10, No.34, 19 August 1852, 297–301, especially 299

[11] See on this in detail the 'Critical Report' of the Complete Edition volume, RSA I/3, 363–389

[12] Letter lost, documented in: *Robert Schumann, Verzeichnis der empfangenen und abgesandten Briefe*, Robert-Schumann-Haus, Zwickau; Archives-Nr.: *4871/VII C, 10–A3*, 'Letters sent', No.2310

V

OAP Original edition of the score

G.M.Meyer jr. (Henry Litolff), Braunschweig, January 1855

Plate number: 1109

Title-page: *OUVERTURE / zu / Shakspeare's Julius Cäsar / für grosses Orchester / componirt von / ROBERT SCHUMANN. / Op. 128. / PARTITUR //* [left:] *No. 1109. //* [centre:] *Eigenthum des Verlegers //* [right:] *Pr. 2 Rthlr. // BRAUNSCHWEIG / bei G. M. Meyer jr (Henry Litolff) //* [left:] *London bei J. J. Ewer & Co //* [right:] *New-York bei Fr. Meyer. // Lith Inst. v. A. Wehrt.*

OAP was advertised together with the other published editions (OAO as well as the piano arrangements for two and four hands) on 20 November 1854 in the *Signale für die musikalische Welt* as *Novitäten der letzten Woche* ['New Publications of the Last Week'], but then advertised as 'published' only on 2 January 1855,[13] just as in the January edition of the *Hofmeister Monatsbericht*.[14]

OAO Original edition of the orchestral parts

G.M.Meyer jr. (Henry Litolff), Braunschweig, January 1855

Plate number: 1136

Vc./Cb. engraved together. Only Vl. I with title-page: *OUVERTURE / zu / SHAKSPEARE'S / JULIUS CÄSAR / COMPONIRT / VON / ROB. SCHUMANN. / OP. 128. //* [left:] *Für grosses Orchester. / Partitur 2 Thlr.__ „ / Stimmen 4 Thlr.__ „ //* [right:] *Für Pianoforte / zu 2 Händen __ „ 16 gGr. / zu 4 Händen 1 Thlr. __ „ // Eigenthum des Verlegers. / BRAUNSCHWEIG, BEI G. M. MEYER Jʀ. (HENRY LITOLFF). //* [left:] *LONDON, BEI J. J. EWER & Co. //* [right:] *NEW-YORK, BEI FR. MEYER. // Vierhändiger Klavierauszug von Woldemar Bargiel.*

OAO was advertised with the other published editions (OAP as well as the piano arrangements for two and four hands) on 20 November 1854 in *Signale* as 'New Publications of the Last Week', but then advertised as 'published' only on 2 January 1855, just as in the January edition of the *Hofmeister Monatsbericht*.

KL List of corrections for the printed score (OAP)[15]

Endenich, January 1855

D-Zsch; Archives-No.: *4871, V, 6, 3–A3*

Clara Schumann reported to Joseph Joachim in a letter of 12 January 1855,[16] that the previous day at Johannes Brahms's visit, Schumann had shown that he was extremely annoyed about the incorrectness of OAP and had sent a 'sheet of corrections' (=KL) along with him.

OAOT Original edition of the orchestral parts, title issue

G.M.Meyer jr. (Henry Litolff), Braunschweig, 1856

Plate number: 1136.

Vc./Cb. engraved together. Only Vl. I with title-page: *OUVERTURE / zu / SHAKSPEARE'S / JULIUS CÄSAR / COMPONIRT / VON / ROB. SCHUMANN. / OP. 128. //* [left:] *Für grosses Orchester. / Partitur 2 Thlr.__ „ / Stimmen 4 Thlr.__ „ //* [right:] *Für Pianoforte / zu 2 Händen __ „ 16 gGr. / zu 4 Händen 1 Thlr. __ „ // Eigenthum des Verlegers. / BRAUNSCHWEIG, HENRY LITOLFF'S VERLAG. //* [left:] *PARIS, / ENOCH PÈRE ET FILS. //* [centre:] *BRUXELLES, / ENOCH PÈRE ET FILS. //*

---

[13] *Signale*, Vol.12, No.47, 20 November 1854, 381, and Vol.13, No.2, 2 January 1855, 15

[14] Friedrich Hofmeister, et al. [ed.], *Musikalisch-Litterarischer Monats-Bericht neuer Musikalien, musikalischer Schriften und Abbildungen* [...] (Leipzig, 1839ff., here: Vol.27 or 5ᵗʰ Issue, Vol.4, No. 1, January 1855), 688

[15] Facsimile in: *Robert Schumann in Endenich (1854–1856): Krankenakten, Briefzeugnisse und zeitgenössische Berichte*, ed. Bernhard R.Appel, with a preface by Aribert Reimann (Mainz, etc., 2006, *Schumann Forschungen*, 11), 535, with commentary, 534

[16] Robert-Schumann-Haus, Zwickau; Archives-No.: *6307-A2*

[right:] *LONDON, / L. SCHUTTE & CO. // Vierhändiger Klavierauszug von Woldemar Bargiel.*
In content, this edition is identical with OAO.

Schumann's *Ouverture zu Shakespeare's Julius Cäsar* Op.128 appeared in print at his instigation in his lifetime in the form of the original editions OAP and OAO as well as the piano arrangements for two and four hands. For all four editions Schumann had sent the publishing house manuscript sources as models. Their whereabouts is not known and thus they cannot be consulted as reference sources. It is problematical that there is no evidence that Schumann had corrected the prints before publication; however, OAP proved upon Schumann's inspection in Endenich shortly after its appearance to be incorrect. The critical inspection and the comparison of OAP and OAO lead likewise to this outcome for both publications. Thus, for the orchestral version, as main sources OAP can only serve the present edition in combination with Schumann's correction list KL and OAO, especially with respect to phrasing, articulation and, as appropriate, also dynamic markings.

The present edition, following the editorial guidelines of the New Schumann Edition, is hence based on the text of the original edition of the score OAP in combination with Schumann's correction list KL as well as the original edition of the parts OAO, especially concerning phrasing, articulation and if applicable, also dynamic markings. Fingerings from OAO were adopted as well. Editorial emendations are indicated in the music text by [ ] or broken lines (for slur placement); other interventions and problematic places are documented in the following report, offering an excerpt from the 'Editorial Notes' of the volume of the complete edition.

For two parts that are notated in OAP on one stave (e.g., Ob.), slurs, stems and/or articulation signs are, as typical of the time, frequently notated only once. Corresponding signs for each of the other parts are normally added tacitly. Also, the doubled stemming for divided voices is not consistently implemented. Triplet signs appear, sometimes with a slur, sometimes with two slurs. Single slurs notated with triplet numbers, etc., were interpreted as grouping slurs and given within brackets in the edition only in unclear cases.

In OAP and OAO (*de-*)*crescendo* hairpins as well as other dynamic markings are repeatedly placed non-uniformly. The discrepancies of the individual parts from the resolution in the edition standardised as far as possible are each listed in the report. In OAP as well as also in OAO hairpins sometimes end just before the subsequent note; the overall length and also parallel parts show as a rule that the (*de-*)*crescendo* should still obtain for these notes, but for the same place span in the bar the hairpin is slightly displaced in the single parts. Therefore such places were standardised without comment.

In OAP as well as also in OAO drum rolls are notated non-uniformly: either as *tr* (with or without ⁓⁓⁓), or by ⸓ added to notes. A method that could indicate a difference for instance of rhythmically-metrically free drum rolls as opposed to exact demisemiquaver values is not discernible. In spite of that, standardisation was dispensed with. The edition follows OAO in these cases.

Armin Koch
Translation: Margit L. McCorkle

VORWORT

Von Robert Schumann sind insgesamt neun vollständig komponierte, als Ouvertüren betitelte Werke für Orchester überliefert. Die meisten davon sind auf seine Initiative hin zumindest auch eigenständig aufgeführt und veröffentlicht worden oder waren immerhin für Aufführung und Veröffentlichung vorgesehen. Mehrheitlich weisen sie im Titel ausdrücklich ein außermusikalisches Sujet bzw. einen musikalischen Bezug auf. Sonderfälle bilden der frühe Versuch *Ouverture et Chor* von 1822/23 (RSW Anhang I9, von Schumann nicht veröffentlicht) und *Ouverture, Scherzo und Finale* op. 52. Letzteres ist das einzige Ouvertüren-Werk ohne explizit äußerlichen Bezug.

Drei der Ouvertüren entstammen größeren Werkzusammenhängen: der Oper *Genoveva* op. 81, dem von Schumann als „Dramatisches Gedicht" bezeichneten *Manfred* op. 115 sowie den *Scenen aus Goethes Faust* (postum veröffentlicht, WoO 3). Die Ouvertüren zu *Genoveva* (entstanden 1847, gedruckt 1850) und *Manfred* (entstanden 1848, gedruckt 1852), die Schumann beide vor den übrigen Teilen des jeweiligen Werkes komponiert hatte, ließ der Komponist selbst auch als eigenständige Werke drucken und aufführen, für die – als letzter Teil des Werks entstandene – Ouvertüre zu den *Faust-Scenen* gibt es diesbezüglich keine ausdrücklichen Hinweise. Drei weitere, innerhalb nur eines Jahres entstandene Ouvertüren sind – wie auch die *Fest-Ouverture mit Gesang über das Rheinweinlied* op. 123 – ohne größeren Werkzusammenhang überliefert, also als reine Konzertouvertüren anzusehen. Zwar gingen zweien davon Überlegungen zu einer Opern- bzw. Liederspielkomposition voraus (*Ouverture zur Braut von Messina von Fr. v. Schiller* op. 100, entstanden Ende 1850/Anfang 1851, gedruckt 1851, und *Ouverture zu Goethes Hermann und Dorothea*, entstanden Ende 1851, postum als op. 136 veröffentlicht). Es sind jedoch keinerlei musikalische Quellen bekannt, die die Ouvertüren ergänzen

würden. Für die *Ouverture zu Shakespeares Julius Cäsar* op. 128 (entstanden Frühjahr 1851, gedruckt 1854/55) sind keine solchen Überlegungen dokumentiert. Die *Rheinweinlied-Ouvertüre* unterscheidet sich grundsätzlich von den übrigen, da sie als *Fest-Ouverture* – komponiert für das Niederrheinische Musikfest 1853 – einer anderen Gattung angehört.

Aus der Zeit der Komposition der Ouvertüre zur *Braut von Messina* stammt ein Tagebucheintrag Clara Schumanns über ihren Mann:[1] „Die Idee, zu mehreren der schönsten Trauerspiele Ouvertüren zu schreiben, hat ihn so begeistert, daß sein Genius wieder von Musik übersprudelt." Im sogenannten *Düsseldorfer Merkbuch* hielt Schumann neben einer langen Reihe von Trauerspielen auch eine Liste für die Idee eines – wie er in einem Brief schrieb[2] – *Cyklus der Ouvertüren* fest:[3] als Nummern 1–4 die zu *Genoveva, Braut von Messina, Julius Cäsar* und *Manfred*. Für den *Cyklus* war nie ausdrücklich von einer Beschränkung auf Trauerspiele als Sujets die Rede und so konnte Schumann später als Nummer 5 die Ouvertüre zu *Hermann und Dorothea* hinzufügen. Der Plan wurde jedoch nicht verwirklicht.

Zum vorliegenden Werk

Die *Ouverture zu Shakespeare's Julius Cäsar* op. 128 komponierte Robert Schumann inner-

[1] Berthold Litzmann, *Clara Schumann. Ein Künstlerleben. Nach Tagebüchern und Briefen*, Bd. II: *Ehejahre 1840–1856*, Leipzig [6]1920, S. 259.
[2] Brief Schumanns an den Verlag C. F. Peters, 24. März 1851, Heinrich-Heine-Institut, Düsseldorf; Akzessions-Nr.: *91.5045/1*. Schumanns Briefwechsel mit dem Verlag ist gedruckt in: *Briefwechsel Robert und Clara Schumanns mit Leipziger Verlegern III*, hg. von Petra Dießner, Irmgard Knechtges-Obrecht und Thomas Synofzik, Köln 2008 (*Schumann Briefedition*, III/3).
[3] *Robert Schumann. Düsseldorfer Merkbuch*, Robert-Schumann-Haus, Zwickau; Archiv-Nr.: *4871, VII, C, 7–A3*, S. 7.

halb weniger Tage.[4] Am 23. Januar 1851 begann er mit dem Entwurf und schloss die Partitur am 2. Februar ab,[5] nicht einmal drei Wochen, nachdem er seine Ouvertüre zu Friedrich Schillers *Braut von Messina* op. 100 fertiggestellt hatte. Während letztere durch Überlegungen zu einem möglichen Opernstoff angeregt wurde, ist für die Ouvertüre zu William Shakespeares *Julius Cäsar* kein solch konkreter Impuls bekannt.

Schumann hatte die Ouvertüre zunächst für den Konzertwinter 1851/52 eingeplant,[6] dann aber doch nicht aufgeführt. Stattdessen wurde das Werk im *Großen Vocal- und Instrumental-Concert* am dritten Tag des Düsseldorfer *Großen Gesangfests* (1. bis 4. August 1852) gespielt.[7] Schumann war in dieser Zeit gesundheitlich stark angeschlagen. Sein Schwager Woldemar Bargiel, den Schumann mit der Erstellung des Klavierauszugs zu vier Händen beauftragt hatte, nutzte die Proben sowie die Aufführung, um das Werk besser kennenzulernen. In seinem Tagebuch des Sommers 1852 notierte er für den ersten Probentag, den 30. Juli:[8]

Endlich waren die Musiker zum Proben versammelt; das Orchester war noch sehr dürftig besetzt und manches[?] Instrument fehlte ganz, indessen ging es doch besser als ich dachte; nach dem 3ten mal klang die Beethovensche Ouverture op. 124 ganz passabel, die Sch[umann]sche allerdings ein bischen kraus, und erst zuletzt, als Sch.[umann] selbst dirigirte, kam ein ordentlicher Zusammenhang hinein. Tausch hatte zuerst dirigirt und ich muß gestehn, daß er der Sache [nicht?] ganz gewachsen schien. Die Cäsarouvertüre hat mich mächtig angesprochen und ich wage[?] nichts daran zu tadeln, da die meisten auffallenden

Stellen grade die tiefsten in der Erfindung sind und ein oberflächliches Urtheil dazu gehört, kurz drüber abzusprechen; sie wird gewiß die großartigste Wirkung hervorbringen. Sch[umann], der seine Ouverture erst mit anhörte, konnte es sich nicht versagen zuletzt selbst den Stab in die Hand zu nehmen und ich habe mich gefreut mit welcher Umsicht und Energie er dirigirte, noch mehr aber darüber, daß <ihn> es ihn ganz gesund schien gemacht zu haben, denn ich traf ihn in bester Stimmung bei dem Abendbrod, so wünsch ich mir, daß die Festtage unter seiner Leitung dahin gehen.

Die Rezension des Musikfestes in der *Berliner Musik-Zeitung Echo* vom 15. August 1852 unterstellt für das Konzert allgemein eine mangelhafte Vorbereitung des Orchesters sowie ein Ungleichgewicht von Bläsern und Streichern und kritisiert speziell die uraufgeführte Ouvertüre.[9] Ganz anders fiel die umfangreiche Rezension der Musikzeitung *Signale für die musikalische Welt* über das Gesangsfest wenige Tage später, am 19. August, aus. Die Betonung der exakten Ausführung und die Erwähnung problematischer Akustik der provisorisch gebauten *Tonhalle* deuten darauf hin, dass der Bericht nicht zuletzt auf die Kritik der *Berliner Musik-Zeitung Echo* reagierte.[10]

Revisionsbericht[11]

Bis auf einen Entwurf in Particell-Form sowie eine nur wenige Takte umfassende und gestrichene Ausschrift der Flötenstimme sind keine handschriftlichen Quellen überliefert. Die am 14. September 1853[12] an Henry Litolff, den Eigentümer des Verlags G. M. Meyer in Braunschweig, geschickten Stichvorlagen verblieben offenbar im Verlag und sind verschollen. Für

---

4 Eine ausführliche Darstellung der *Werkgeschichte* findet sich im Band der Gesamtausgabe *Robert Schumann. Neue Ausgabe sämtlicher Werke*, Serie I, Werkgruppe 3 (RSA I/3) mit den Orchesterfassungen der Ouvertüren, S. 339–362.
5 Vgl. *Robert Schumann. Projectenbuch,* Robert-Schumann-Haus, Zwickau; Archiv-Nr.: *4871, VII, C,8–A3,* S. 59.
6 Siehe *Düsseldorfer Merkbuch,* S. 21.
7 Vgl. *Städtischer Männergesangverein zu Düsseldorf. GROSSES GESANGFEST. GESANGWETTSTREIT, COMPOSITIONSKAMPF, Concert und Grosses Künstlerfest der Gesellschaft Malkasten am 1., 2., 3. und 4. August 1852. Programm und Fest-Ordnung. Ehrenpreise, Texte der Gesänge, Namens-Verzeichniss sämmtlicher Mitwirkenden,* Düsseldorf [1852].
8 Robert-Schumann-Haus, Zwickau; Archiv-Nr.: *2008.037–A3,* Eintrag zum 30. Juli 1852, S. [31–34].

9 Vgl. „,– W. –", „,Das Sänger- und Musikfest in Düsseldorf am 1–3. August d. J.", in: *Berliner Musik-Zeitung Echo,* 2. Jg., Nr. 33, 15. August 1852, S. 259–261, besonders S. 259f.
10 Anon. [= Wilhelm Joseph von Wasielewski], „Das Düsseldorfer Gesangfest", in: *Signale,* 10. Jg., Nr. 34, 19. August 1852, S. 297–301, besonders S. 299.
11 Siehe dazu ausführlich den *Kritischen Bericht* des genannten Gesamtausgaben-Bandes RSA I/3, S. 363–389.
12 Brief verschollen, belegt in: *Robert Schumann, Verzeichnis der empfangenen und abgesandten Briefe,* Robert-Schumann-Haus, Zwickau; Archiv-Nr.: *4871/VII C, 10–A3, Abgesandte Briefe,* Nr. 2310.

die vorliegende Ausgabe relevante überlieferte Quellen:

OAP   Originalausgabe der Partitur
G. M. Meyer jr. (Henry Litolff), Braunschweig, Januar 1855
Plattennummer: 1109
Titelblatt: *OUVERTURE / zu / Shakspeare's Julius Cäsar / für grosses Orchester / componirt von / ROBERT SCHUMANN. / Op. 128. / PARTITUR //* [links:] *№. 1109. //* [mittig:] *Eigenthum des Verlegers //* [rechts:] *Pr. 2 Rthlr. // BRAUNSCHWEIG / bei G. M. Meyer jr (Henry Litolff) //* [links:] *London bei J. J. Ewer & Cᵒ* [rechts:] *New-York bei Fr. Meyer. // Lith Inst. v. A. Wehrt.*
OAP wurde mit den anderen Druckausgaben (OAO sowie Klavierauszüge zu zwei und vier Händen) am 20. November 1854 in den *Signalen für die musikalische Welt* gesammelt als *Novitäten der letzten Woche*, dann aber erst am 2. Januar 1855 als *erschienen* angezeigt,[13] ebenso in der Januar-Ausgabe von *Hofmeisters Monatsbericht.*[14]

OAO   Originalausgabe der Orchesterstimmen
G. M. Meyer jr. (Henry Litolff), Braunschweig, Januar 1855
Plattennummer: 1136
Vc./Kb. gemeinsam gestochen. Nur Vl. I mit Titelblatt: *OUVERTURE / zu / SHAKSPEARE'S / JULIUS CÄSAR / COMPONIRT / VON / ROB. SCHUMANN. / OP. 128. //* [links:] *Für grosses Orchester. / Partitur 2 Thlr.__ „ / Stimmen 4 Thlr.__ „ //* [rechts:] *Für Pianoforte / zu 2 Händen __ „ 16 gGr. / zu 4 Händen 1 Thlr. __ „ // Eigenthum des Verlegers. / BRAUNSCHWEIG, BEI G. M. MEYER Jᴿ. (HENRY LITOLFF). //* [links:] *LONDON, BEI J. J. EWER & Cᴼ· //* [rechts:] *NEW-YORK, BEI*

FR. MEYER. // Vierhändiger Klavierauszug von Woldemar Bargiel.
OAO wurde mit den anderen Druckausgaben (OAP sowie Klavierauszüge zu zwei und vier Händen) am 20. November 1854 in den *Signalen* gesammelt als *Novitäten der letzten Woche*, dann aber erst am 2. Januar 1855 als *erschienen* angezeigt, ebenso in der Januar-Ausgabe von *Hofmeisters Monatsbericht.*

KL   Korrekturliste zum Partiturdruck (OAP)[15]
Endenich, Januar 1855
D-Zsch; Archiv-Nr.: *4871,V,6,3–A3*
Clara Schumann berichtet in einem Brief an Joseph Joachim vom 12. Januar 1855,[16] Schumann habe sich Johannes Brahms gegenüber bei dessen Besuch am Vortag äußerst verärgert über die Fehlerhaftigkeit von OAP gezeigt und Brahms einen *Bogen von Correcturen* (= KL) mitgegeben.

OAOT   Originalausgabe der Orchesterstimmen, Titelauflage
G. M. Meyer jr. (Henry Litolff), Braunschweig, 1856
Plattennummer: 1136.
Vc./Kb. gemeinsam gestochen. Nur Vl. I mit Titelblatt: *OUVERTURE / zu / SHAKSPEARE'S / JULIUS CÄSAR / COMPONIRT / VON / ROB. SCHUMANN. / OP. 128. //* [links:] *Für grosses Orchester. / Partitur 2 Thlr.__ „ / Stimmen 4 Thlr.__ „ //* [rechts:] *Für Pianoforte / zu 2 Händen __ „ 16 gGr. / zu 4 Händen 1 Thlr. __ „ // Eigenthum des Verlegers. / BRAUNSCHWEIG, HENRY LITOLFF'S VERLAG. //* [links:] *PARIS, / ENOCH PÈRE ET FILS. //* [mittig:] *BRUXELLES, / ENOCH PÈRE ET FILS. //* [rechts:] *LONDON, / L. SCHUTTE & CO.*

---

13 *Signale*, 12. Jg., Nr. 47, 20. November 1854, S. 381, bzw. 13. Jg., Nr. 2, 2. Januar 1855, S. 15.
14 Friedrich Hofmeister, et al. [Hg.], *Musikalisch-Litterarischer Monats-Bericht neuer Musikalien, musikalischer Schriften und Abbildungen [...]*, Leipzig 1839ff., hier: 27. Jg. oder 5. Folge, 4. Jg., Nr. 1, Januar 1855, S. 688.

15 Faksimiliert in: *Robert Schumann in Endenich (1854–1856): Krankenakten, Briefzeugnisse und zeitgenössische Berichte*, hg. von Bernhard R. Appel, mit einem Vorwort von Aribert Reimann, Mainz usw. 2006 (*Schumann Forschungen*, 11), S. 535 mit Kommentar S. 534.
16 Robert-Schumann-Haus, Zwickau; Archiv-Nr.: *6307-A2.*

X

// Vierhändiger Klavierauszug von Woldemar Bargiel.
Inhaltlich ist diese Ausgabe identisch mit OAO.

Schumanns *Ouverture zu Shakespeare's Julius Cäsar* op. 128 ist auf seine Veranlassung hin zu seinen Lebzeiten in Form der Originalausgaben OAP und OAO sowie der Klavierauszüge zu zwei und vier Händen im Druck erschienen. Für alle vier Ausgaben hatte Schumann handschriftliche Quellen als Vorlagen an den Verlag geschickt. Über ihren Verbleib ist nichts bekannt und so können sie nicht als Referenzquellen herangezogen werden. Problematisch ist, dass es keinen Hinweis darauf gibt, dass Schumann die Drucke vor der Veröffentlichung korrigiert hätte und sich OAP bei Schumanns Durchsicht in Endenich kurz nach ihrem Erscheinen als fehlerhaft erwies. Die kritische Sichtung und der Vergleich von OAP und OAO führen für beide Drucke ebenfalls zu diesem Ergebnis. Für die Orchesterfassung bilden daher OAP in Verbindung mit Schumanns Korrekturliste KL und insbesondere im Hinblick auf Phrasierung, Artikulation und ggf. auch dynamische Angaben OAO die Hauptquellen der vorliegenden Edition.

Der vorliegenden Ausgabe, die den Editionsrichtlinien der Neuen Schumann-Gesamtausgabe folgt, liegen daher der Text des Partitur-Originaldrucks OAP in Verbindung mit Schumanns Korrekturliste KL sowie insbesondere im Hinblick auf Phrasierung, Artikulation und ggf. auch dynamische Angaben OAO als Hauptquellen zugrunde. Aus OAO wurden darüber hinaus Fingersätze übernommen. Ergänzungen des Herausgebers sind im Notentext durch [ ] bzw. Strichelung (bei Bogensetzung) kenntlich gemacht; andere Eingriffe und problematische Stellen sind im folgenden Bericht dokumentiert, der einen Auszug aus dem Revisionsbericht des Gesamtausgaben-Bandes bietet.

Bei zwei Stimmen, die in OAP in einem System notiert sind (z. B. Hob.), sind häufig Bögen, Hälse bzw. Artikulationszeichen zeittypisch nur einmal notiert. Entsprechende Zeichen für die jeweils andere Stimme sind in der Edition normalerweise stillschweigend ergänzt. Auch die doppelte Halsung bei geteilten Stimmen ist nicht konsequent durchgeführt. Triolenzeichen erscheinen z. T. mit einem Bogen, z. T. mit zwei Bögen. Einzelne Bögen bei Triolenziffern usw. wurden als Gruppenbögen aufgefasst und in der Edition nur in missverständlichen Fällen als Klammer wiedergegeben.

In OAP und OAO sind (De-)Crescendo-Gabeln sowie andere dynamische Angaben mehrfach uneinheitlich gesetzt. Die Abweichungen der einzelnen Stimmen von der soweit möglich vereinheitlichten Lösung in der Edition sind im Bericht jeweils aufgelistet. Sowohl in OAP als auch in OAO enden Gabeln teilweise knapp vor der Folgenote; die Länge insgesamt und in der Regel auch Parallelstimmen zeigen, dass das (De-)Crescendo noch für diese Noten gelten soll, aber bei gleicher Breite der Gabel der Ort im Takt in den einzelnen Stimmen leicht verschoben ist. Daher wurden solche Stellen ohne Bemerkung vereinheitlicht.

Sowohl in OAP als auch OAO sind Paukenwirbel uneinheitlich notiert: zum einen als *tr* mit oder ohne Wirbel-Wellenlinie, zum anderen durch drei den Noten hinzugefügte Tremolostriche. Eine Systematik, die auf eine Unterscheidung etwa von rhythmisch-metrisch freiem Wirbel gegenüber exakten Zweiunddreißigstelwerten deuten könnte, ist nicht erkennbar. Trotzdem wurde auf eine Vereinheitlichung verzichtet. Die Edition folgt in diesen Fällen OAO.

Armin Koch

Einzelanmerkungen

Takt(e)	Stimme(n)	Anmerkung
		Titelblatt OAP, OAO: *Shakspeare* statt *Shakespeare*
7, 8	Vl. I	OAP, OAO: 2. ZZ  ; für die Edition als beschleunigende Figur aufgefasst und 1.–3. Note als Triole gekennzeichnet; in den Klavierauszügen jedoch als
12	Fg.	OAP, OAO: 4. Note mit >; OAO: ohne ⸺; in der Edition > mit Blick auf die übrigen Stimmen und Parallelstelle T. 126 nicht berücksichtigt
16	Pk.	OAP:

nach dieser Lesart und da auch in OAO kein Haltebogen notiert ist, ist es denkbar, den Wirbel als nur für ♩ geltend zu verstehen (vgl. auch T. 130)

| 20–23, 134–137 | Hob., Clar. | OAP, OAO: Bogensetzung problematisch (vgl. auch Fg.); für die Edition unter Auflösung der Girlandenbögen weitgehend beibehalten; T. 22–23, Hob. 2, OAO: 2. Bogenende erst zu 4. ZZ; in der Edition wegen Tonrepetition zu 3. ZZ gesetzt. In den Quellen untereinander abweichend für Hob. und Clar. |

T. 20–23, OAP:

T. 20–23, OAO:

T. 134–137, OAP:

T. 134–137, OAO:

Möglicherweise waren jene Takte in der verschollenen autographen Partitur nicht (vollständig) ausgeschrieben – insbesondere die Reprisentakte 134–137 –, so dass die Abweichungen der Parallelstelle durch Ausschrift oder Stich zustande kamen und dadurch weniger Gewicht hätten. Denkbar wäre daher eine Angleichung der Bogensetzung in den Stimmen aufgrund der gleichen Figuren.

22	V.-Hn. 1	OAP: ohne ⎯⎯ ; OAO: ⎯⎯ 2.–3. Note; in der Edition angeglichen an die übrigen Stimmen; vgl. T. 136
27–28	Fg.	OAP Fg. 1, 2 und OAO Fg. 1: mit zusätzlichem Bogen T. 27, 1. Note–T. 28, 1. Note; OAO: Bogensetzung Fg. 2 ⎮ ♩ ♩ ♩ o ⎮; in der Edition taktübergreifende Bögen mit Blick auf die anderen Bläserstimmen sowie die Parallelstelle T. 141–142 nicht berücksichtigt
53	Pos. 1	OAP: ^ statt >; OAO: ohne >; in der Edition analog den übrigen Blechbläserstimmen als > gesetzt
55	Pos. 2, 3	OAP, OAO (Pos. 2) 1. Note mit *sf* statt >; in der Edition entsprechend OAO Pos. 3 sowie den übrigen Blechbläserstimmen im Umfeld gesetzt
61	Fg., Vc., B.	OAP, OAO: ⎯⎯ statt *cresc.*; für die Edition analog den übrigen Stimmen im Umfeld in *cresc.* geändert
66	Va., Vc., B.	OAP, OAO: > zu 1. Note statt ⎯⎯; in der Edition an die übrigen Stimmen angeglichen
89	Hob.	OAP: ohne *cresc.*; OAO: *cresc.* zu 4. ZZ statt 3. ZZ; in der Edition angeglichen an übrige Stimmen
101	Fg.	OAP: ohne ⎯⎯ ⎯⎯; OAO: ⎯⎯ für T. 101, ⎯⎯ für T. 102; in der Edition ⎯⎯ ⎯⎯ analog den übrigen Stimmen gesetzt
	Vc.	OAP: ⎯⎯ für T. 101, Höhe 3. Taktachtel–4. ZZ, und ⎯⎯ für T. 102, Höhe 3. Taktachtel–Höhe 6. Taktachtel; OAO: ⎯⎯ ⎯⎯ T. 101, 2.–4. ZZ, und T. 102, Höhe 2.–4. ZZ; in der Edition ⎯⎯ ⎯⎯ analog den übrigen Stimmen gesetzt
	B.	OAP: ohne ⎯⎯ ⎯⎯; OAO: ⎯⎯ für T. 101, 2.–4. ZZ, und ⎯⎯ für T. 102, Höhe 2.–4. ZZ; in der Edition ⎯⎯ ⎯⎯ analog den übrigen Stimmen gesetzt

+108–109	Clar., Fg.	OAP: *f* zu T. 108, 1. Note, statt zu T. +108; OAO: *sf* zu T. 108, 1. Note, und T. 109, 1. Note, statt *f* zu T. +108; in der Edition ausgeglichen an W.-Hn. und V.-Trp.
108–109	Pk.	OAP, OAO: in beiden Quellen übereinstimmend von den übrigen Stimmen abweichende Dynamik; möglicherweise versehentlich nicht korrigiert
111	Clar. 2	OAP, OAO: 3. ZZ notiert c¹ statt klingend c¹ (notiert d¹)
113–114	Pk.	OAP: OAO:

für die Edition Wellenlinie wie in OAO gesetzt, die Bogensetzung aber aufgrund der doppelten Fermate aus OAP übernommen

116	Pos. 1, 2	OAP, OAO: *dim.* erst zu 2. Takthälfte; in der Edition analog den übrigen Stimmen vorgezogen
	Pos. 3	OAP, OAO: 1.–2. Note mit Bogen; in der Edition mit Blick auf Pos. 1, 2 sowie Parallelstelle T. 2 (trotz Änderung der Dynamik) nicht berücksichtigt
117–118	Fl.	OAP, OAO: mit zusätzlichem Bogen T. 117, 1. Note, bis T. 118, 1. Note; in der Edition mit Blick auf Hob. 1, Fg. nicht berücksichtigt
121	Va., Vc.	OAP, OAO: *p* erst zu 2. Takthälfte; in der Edition mit Blick auf die Bläserstimmen vorgezogen
123	Tb., Pk.	OAP, OAO: *sf* statt *f*; in der Edition angeglichen an die übrigen Stimmen
130	Pk.	OAP: ohne Wellenlinie; nach dieser Lesart und da auch in OAO kein Haltebogen notiert ist, ist es denkbar, den Wirbel als nur für ♩ geltend zu verstehen (vgl. auch T. 16)
133	Pos. 1, 2	OAP, OAO: ^ statt >; geändert mit Blick auf die übrigen Bläser
134–137	V.-Hn. 1	OAP:

OAO:

die Edition folgt OAO

136	V.-Hn. 1	OAP, OAO: siehe Anmerkung zu T. 134–137; in der Edition ⸺ angeglichen an die übrigen Stimmen; vgl. T. 22
137	Hob. 2	OAP, OAO: 4. ZZ ♮a¹ statt f¹; in der Edition aus Stimmführungsgründen angeglichen an Parallelstelle T. 23
148	Fl.	OAP, OAO: 2. Bogen bis letzte Note; in der Edition angeglichen an Hob., Clar. mit Blick auf die Parallelstelle T. 46
155–157	V.-Hn., W.-Hn.	OAP, OAO: jeweils ^ statt > (außer W.-Hn. 1, OAO); angeglichen an V.-Trp. und Pos. entsprechend Parallelstelle T. 53–55

157–158	Hob., Clar.	OAP, OAO: *p* erst T. 158, 1. Note; in der Edition *p* vorgezogen und Bögen ergänzt analog T. 55–56
	Clar. 1	OAO: ohne *p*
159	Pos. 1	OAP, OAO: > statt *sf*; *sf* analog Hn. gesetzt
176	Fg. 2, V.-Hn.	OAP, OAO: 4. ZZ ♩♩ statt ♫; in der Edition angeglichen an Vc., B.; vgl. T. 74
181	Vc.	OAP, OAO: *pp* statt *p*; in der Edition angepasst an die Dynamik der übrigen Stimmen
184	Vl. I, Va.	OAP, OAO: *cresc.* erst zu 2. Note
184, 186	B.	OAP: ohne *cresc.*; OAO: *cresc.* erst zu 2. ZZ
210	Fg.	OAP: ohne Dynamik
		OAO: 1.–3. ZZ ⸺ , *p* für 4. ZZ
212	V.-Trp. 2	OAP, OAO: 4. ZZ (notiert) e statt d
	Pos. 1	OAP, OAO: Bogenende erst bei T. 213, 1. ZZ
	Pos. 1, 2	OAP: ohne *cresc.*; OAO: *cresc.* erst zu 3. ZZ; für die Edition angeglichen an übrige Stimmen
	Vl. II	OAP, OAO: 3. ZZ d^1 statt g^1; plausibler erscheint die Parallelführung mit Hob. und Clar. 2; so in der Edition umgesetzt
217	V.-Hn.	OAP, OAO: 1. ZZ mit *sf*; in der Edition mit Blick auf die übrigen Stimmen nicht berücksichtigt

OVERTURE
to Shakespeare's Julius Caesar

Robert Schumann
(1810–1856)
Op. 128

Edited by Armin Koch
© 2014 Ernst Eulenburg Ltd, London
and Ernst Eulenburg & Co GmbH, Mainz

3

5

6

Etwas schneller ♩ = 104

12

14

16

20

21

22

26

32

Tempo wie zu Anfang

38

39

40

52

53